Counting the Ways

Counting the Ways

Poems by

Sharon Rhutasel-Jones

© 2025 Sharon Rhutasel-Jones. All rights reserved.
This material may not be reproduced in any form, published,
reprinted, recorded, performed, broadcast,
rewritten or redistributed without
the explicit permission of Sharon Rhutasel-Jones.
All such actions are strictly prohibited by law.

Cover design by Shay Culligan
Cover image by Sharon Rhutasel-Jones
Author photo by Sharon Rhutasel-Jones

ISBN: 978-1-63980-838-0

Kelsay Books
502 South 1040 East, A-119
American Fork, Utah 84003
Kelsaybooks.com

Acknowledgments

I'm not exactly sure when I first started writing poetry, but I remember a former student Phyllis Rogers saying, "You always assigned us to write poetry, so now it's your turn." As a result, I produced some awful poems and then progressed enough to get a few pieces published.

As to haiku, I also don't remember how I first started; however, my friend Sondra Byrnes, the author of *An Unlikely Truth*, had something to do with it. These days, Sondra and two other friends, Alanna Burke and Charlie Trumbull meet on zoom once a week to critique each other's poems. We laugh and have a joyous time as we make suggestions.

Haibun in a completely different matter. As it's one of my favorite forms of poetry to write, I'm grateful to Matsuo Basho for creating it in the seventeenth century.

Each poem in this book is a verbal counting the ways the magnificent natural world and the people in it appear to me. Hence its title.

Most of the haiku and haibun in this book have previously appeared in *Bottle Rockets, Frogpond, Hedgerow,* or *Modern Haiku*. Longer poems have appeared in *Bearing the Mask, Southwestern Poets Anthology,* and *Weaving the Terrain*.

*Rather than writing a traditional dedication,
I've written a poem in honor of my niece, Alina,
who died in the fall of 2024*

Woman Warrior

During the priest's interminable going on and on
I think of the travel bag Alina gave me
The one made of green fabric a Bolivian woman wove
To help support her family
Road trips always mean it will come along
Like a trusted companion

I love the feel of its fabric
Soft as Alina's curly hair
And I love that she gave it to me
Though we hardly knew each other
I will remember my niece's bravery
Each time I take it down to pack

When Alina and her dad
Not really her dad, really my brother Tom
Went out to eat the first time with my husband, sons, and me
People stared
"She's so used to it, she doesn't notice," Tom explained

The child of an out-of-the-picture Indio father
And a Mexican mother
Her black curly hair and brown, almost black, eyes
Pronounced her a striking beauty
By the time she was four

Then tragedy struck a blow so harsh
None of us could imagine its power at first
Nor could we imagine
Alina would transform into a warrior

When Tom married Alina's mother Elaine
Their only honeymoon
A weeklong stay in Houston
Where Alina was admitted to MD Anderson
For the first of more than 30 surgeries
That stunted her growth and affected her vocal chords
So that her voice sounded like Alvin and the Chipmunks

As the years of her ongoing battle with cancer passed
Alina graduated with a degree in occupational therapy
Marriage, like a melting snowflake, eluded her
But she insisted on fighting a years-long battle
With the legal system to adopt
When at last Reyna, the child of an heroin-addict mother
Officially became my niece's child
Tom, who had adopted Alina, became Dad

After the funeral, I repacked my green travel bag
On the drive home, I thought about Alina's friends' tributes
Most of all, I thought of her courage
In spite of the pain that followed her like a stalker
And of Reyna without the woman warrior she clung to
When Alina brought her home

Contents

I. Persona Poems and Other Long Poems

Cockroaches and the Closet	21
Padre Martínez Goes to Heaven	22
Bluegrass Holiday	24
Calls	27
Dancing in the Graveyard	30
Adobes and Understanding	32
A Belizean Fairy Tale	34
Caring	36
We Didn't Go to Paris	37
Waiting for Words	38
Desert Lovers	40
For Jeanne Who Dreams Horses	42
For Jeanne Who Loved Back	44
High Desert Evenings	46
Pronouns	47
Simple Things	48
Desperate Glory	49
Without You	50
Wild Horses and Old Men	51
Ariel's Wedding Poem	52
Boundaries	53
Crocuses and A Poem	54

II. Haiku

III. Haibun

Paper Bags	79
Belongings	80
Things Not Understood	81
Papa Married an Anglo	83
A New Nose	84
The Witness	85
Desperation	86
The Gamble	87
Veterans' Home	88
Just the Two of Us	89
The Promises They Made	90

IV. Tankas

I. Persona Poems and Other Long Poems

Persona poems are written as though the subject of the poem is actually speaking. "Cockroaches and the Closet" is written in the voice of my dear friend Levi Romero, New Mexico's first Poet Laureate.

Cockroaches and the Closet

Boarding school felt like grit in my eyes
Sometimes, to get rid of it I'd say *"aquí"*
when Miss Benning called roll in math
Her pronunciation of the r's in Romero
sounded like she had cotton balls in her mouth
In her class I'd slide into an S in my desk
and try to rub away the grit that had grown into gravel
No matter how hard I rubbed, the grit stayed put

After lights out, I'd sneak into the janitor's closet
switch on a flashlight and write poetry
When I switched off the light to think
cockroaches danced across the tops of my shoes
Poem by poem, the grit began to dissolve

The cockroaches kept me company
while I read all of Dracula in one night
Then came the assignment for English
When I told my roommate I'd put a poem in my essay about the
Count as a hero
he said, *"Tu estas loco,"* at least ten times

The day my teacher passed the papers back
I stuck mine into a book without looking at the grade
After class, I hid in a bathroom stall
"You're gonna find out sometime, fool," I told myself
as I pulled the essay out of my book
Like the snakes in Medusa's hair, an A squirmed before my eyes

That day, I came out of the closet to stay

Padre Martínez Goes to Heaven

"Hola, Frenchman,
es una sorpresa to find me here, *qué no?*

Excommunicating me didn't work
in spite of your fine statue,
the one of you standing
as straight and slim as an arrow shaft,
looking down your aquiline nose."

"*Ay Dios, Dios,*
Why did you let the Holy Father
send an uppity Frenchman to the land of my heart?
my *Penitente* land where I built schools for my people
and for *los Indios* too?
I even built a printing press.
Casa Martínez became *la iglesia* for my flock
so they could come to pray when they had nowhere else to go."
"'*Vamos a la casa de Dios,*'
they said when they came."

"You, Frenchman, you gave the poor a cathedral
when all they needed were *iglesias* built of mud bricks.
To call the people to mass, you gave them a bell.
I, their bell-shaped *padre,* laughed when I saw it.
And what of *los Penitentes,* those holy men
who kept the faith alive when Rome ignored us?
They inflicted pain on themselves, taking on our sins
as our Lord did,

but in return for their sacrifices
you tried to dishonor them, to keep them from their sacred rites.
'A fool is pleased with his own folly,' my mother used to say."

"Forgive me, Dios,
but *la gente de la tierra de mi corazón* meant nothing to him.
Like a *patrón,* he demanded tithes,
then when the people couldn't pay,
he took away the sacraments.
What kind of priest would do that?"

"You came to our land,
head held high; cold fire in your heart.
You rattled on like a magpie about tithes.
'Blessed are the poor, 'you said.
What about your vow of poverty,
you who lived in a large house and wore fine robes?
If tithes meant so much to you,
why didn't you sell what you had and pay them?

Has the cat got your tongue, Frenchman?"

---

* *Educator, politician, publisher, and priest José Antonio Martínez championed the poor and made the sacraments available before the Catholic Church officially entered New Mexico. After the Church sent Archbishop Jean-Baptiste Lamy to establish the archdiocese of Santa Fe, Martinez refused to collect tithes as per Lamy's orders. As a result, the Archbishop ordered Padre Martínez's excommunication. A beloved figure among his people, Padre Martínez became a nineteenth century folk hero in northern New Mexico.*

Bluegrass Holiday

I.

Long-distance monotony
past Chevy trucks rusting beside ramshackle houses
refinery smoke, stillborn in July heat, winding around teepees for
    tourists
oil town gray crawling up cinderblock walls then
sliding down rain gutters to pour tedium onto sidewalks
cracked to break you mother's back
monotone people reflected in main street windows of cloned cafes

II.

Radio whine
Gimme, gimme, gimme a letter to midnight
hairpin curve, miles of tents crayon pastures of snow-dressed
    mountain green
bumper to bumper
    Beautify Colorado: Buy a Texan a bus ticket
    You can't prepare for war and prevent it at the same time
We slip hungry into the throbbing town
Don't crawfish me baby
sensuous at steel guitar noon
Oklahoma lady, size 18, hawks chile dogs
spicy red stuff slides down my arm to drip designs onto my jeans
We laugh our way toward the music
Balding, overweight bikers stride into the Victorian saloon
at home somehow among relics of the past
Balloons escape into the sky
beyond ubiquitous Coke cups
red, white & blues in the afternoon
beer rain showers
Lady Moon creepin 'down my back stairs
Born just out of wedlock
E=Music times Coors squared
Green cat-eye glasses
    Don't cry; cry blue
Hot pink toenail tappin'
Ole Dan Tucker died with a toothache in his heel
Dance all day; dance all night

III.

Midnight alongside the cemetery
we hear a miner's ghost tuning his fiddle
to join in the bluegrass revival
that keeps his town alive

Calls

3 AM
As though it were a police siren
The phone jars me awake

"They tried to kill me."
Your northern New Mexico roots
Wrap around the words

"They tried to kill me," you repeat
In a voice
As cold as a new razor blade

I wait for more
A long silence, then
"I just needed to tell someone."

"I'm grateful
You have chosen me
So as not to burden your mother," I say

In the bantering back and forth
Of all our years
We've never spoken of your call again

I think of it though
When I remember your fearlessness
On the football field

Nehi, everyone calls you
Your height unimportant
As you streak toward a touchdown

One day
You promise me
"I'm going to make something of myself."

Ten years later
You host a high school reunion party
At your house

As I circulate among them
I wonder whether, having made little of themselves
You sense your classmates' envy

Steve stands
Impaled against a wall
Underneath a Gorman print

"Wishing for another death,"
I tell myself, my heart hurting for him
And his buried football hero dreams

Years later
(I wonder whether you remember)
You push my mother in her wheelchair

We're headed from my son's wedding
To the reception
At a hotel across the way

As I follow
Your kindness
Embraces me

When you have daughters
Your delight radiates
Like the gold in a sunrise

I love watching you
Watching them
On the basketball court

Now, even as a made-it-a-hundred-times-over lawyer
You immediately take
My calls

Dancing in the Graveyard

The dead in New Mexican *camposantos* come out at night
While the grass on the *llano* sleeps
Only in an enchanted land where people throw parties "Just
    because"
Do *los muertos* come out of the grave to dance

In Virginia, two cultures and two thousand miles from home,
We drove past a country cemetery
Where the snow lay like an albino strain of granite
Sealing in the dead

No graveyard parties here among staunch Puritan stock,
I surmised speeding past the icy landscape.
Still, one burial was not enough for the venerable ones
Lying patiently under the snow

Washington, towering above Mount Vernon's fields,
Must surely long to rise again to see the rows of barley on his land,
He, like Adams who followed him,
Left the fields he loved to meld divided factions into a great nation

But these heroes, long dead
And far from free to walk their land,
Come to life again, not in cemeteries
But in the words of somber men writing partial truths about deeds
    long past

In the old ways of *La Raza* of my enchanted land, people leave
    gifts
At the graves of loved ones on *El Dia de Los Muertos,*
The day each year the dead are granted life in death.
The *camposantos* come alive with the laughter of the living and the
    dead
As though God himself commanded a fiesta

My two cultures grapple with what comes after death,
A mystery, more complex than a snowflake's pattern,
One places the dead between the covers of a book
The other plans a graveyard party

I choose the ways of *La Raza de mi padre,*
And dancing in the *camposanto,* if only for a day

Adobes and Understanding

My mind rode a jet stream today
Maybe because it's Friday
Maybe because I'm remembering how
When I lay beside you
As you slipped away, day by quickly day
You smiled in an extraordinary way
As if to say, there are more things in heaven and earth
Than we can understand

But today, the jet's trail streaks through the place
My heart holds you, as if to say
I no longer need to use the past tense
When I speak about you
The quickly one I love who died
On such and such a summer day

Instead I'll say
You live in the adobes
We used to fence in the wildness of our life
In the books you read to me
In the day lilies we were never able to divide
In the roadrunner we named Rio Grande

Instead I'll say
You live in the wild rose
(The one that climbs to the top of the garden gate you built. The
   one
I planted without you.)

Its blooms nod as if to say
You hover somewhere
In the spaces around me
Whispering (quickly) words I feel in the desert air
But cannot understand

---

* In the haibun "The Witness," you'll learn more about my husband David. I wrote "Adobes and Understanding" in his honor.

A Belizean Fairy Tale

Our turquoise tour guide, toned and tan
Didn't object
When a wrinkled, tattooed woman
Put her head on his shoulder and fell asleep

Instead, he gently steadied her
While she slept on, unaware
As we bounced along in a rattletrap Belizean bus
Transporting us to our beachside resort

At the airport, some had frowned when they noticed seaweed
Circling around her arms
Others shook their heads
When she deplaned into a wheelchair

"She'll slow us down," one man said
Others, somewhat solicitous, thought aloud
"She surely should have stayed at home
After all, she clearly isn't well."

Then night settled in over the resort, dragging in the tide
Water crashed high against the shore
Waves washed in and out in sonorous rhythm
While we slept

At dawn, we saw a mermaid strolling along the shore
She glistened as the waves subsided
Her skin, like a rare and radiant opal
Shimmered in the yellow light

Suddenly, we heard our tour guide call to her
Running to follow as she strolled into the sea
We stood, words unformed,
Watching them walk hand in hand farther and farther from shore

When we found our foolish voices
We called to them, begging them to come back
But since they were not the ones dead
The waves dragged them downward
Until they disappeared beneath the sea

Caring

Charles' mother is dying
He pretends he doesn't care

I see his fingers tapping,
Tapping on his desk top while
He thinks of a courteous excuse to give for
Pretending he doesn't care

Then he slips away

Sits alone under the table in my classroom
Because he can't write
What he wants to write and doesn't care
When someone questions his machismo
When he wants to take his skin off after
He lies because
He does care when
He's not done what
He said he'd done and
He knows his lie is
Walking on his knuckles
Crushed white with
Pretending he doesn't care.

Charles's mother is dying
One who's never seen his fingers tapping
Might believe he doesn't care

We Didn't Go to Paris

Last Christmas Eve, for reasons I can't explain
I didn't take you along
As I crossed the Seine, walking to Notre Dame
I didn't stuff you into the back pocket of my jeans
The one you used to put your hand in
Whenever we ambled along
Talking about nothing much
Marking the time of our days
Days when we were both alive
To patterns fallen leaves make on water
To the softest cadence of distant music
Audible to just we two

I didn't go to pray in Notre Dame
Supplications die

On lips left cold by the end of days
Filled with the simplicity of entwined being
When hands trembling with desire

Held water for a baptism so profound
Broken stone faces can't negate it,
Staring sideways across prayers
Across time.

Waiting for Words

Honda, elegant sphinx of a cat,
Sits stone-like beside the terra cotta jar
Sunning himself and thinking
About matters that cats,
Ancient among the gods, share with the stars

He approaches without warning
His courtesy so profound I fail to see him at first
He never interrupts

Understanding that usually when I'm sitting
Words struggling to align properly in my head
Haven't the sense to appear in any kind of order

He sits at my feet for a moment
The question in his green eyes
Waiting to be invited

Before he jumps into my lap
I pat my thigh

He lands with delicate precision
Then turns round and round
Until he gets his position right for each of us
Finally he settles in
Waiting for me to put aside
Whatever words are on my mind
Long enough to scratch his ears

Unlike words that threaten and command
He waits until I'm ready
Once he's settled in my lap
We feel matters he's discussed with the stars
And words, in any order I've arranged them,
Slip silently away

Desert Lovers

Rain rarely keeps its promises in the desert
Thunder, like rumbling boxcars rolling north along the Santa Fe
    line
Receives a cursory hearing
Since everyone knows such talk
Cheap as last season's shoes
Leads to nothing more than dusty spots on windshields

Still, when it does come
Rain's pounding on baked earth bows the resplendent sun
And calls the women to come out
Handmaidens of the sun, wary at first
Catch the rain in cupped hands
Saving it to pour in pots of thick red chile
Or sometimes, when the moon is full, they dance
Faces turned upward
Inviting sensual rain to flow in rivulets
Holy water inching its way toward breasts and waiting thighs
Then, like a fickle lover, it moves on

The sun, knowing exactly how power works
Without warning lifts his head and travels to the mountain top
There he remains
Omnipotent, benevolent, tolerant of indiscretion

Certain the sun is not omniscient
The women respond to his beckoning
But when he turns his back again
They lay aside their gossamer robes
And slip into the presence of the moon

For Jeanne Who Dreams Horses

Sunday morning music
a time of peace, praise and prayer
for both of us

remembering
the Sunday you introduced yourself
I praise the god of friendship

at a run-down adobe bakery
we sat outside
your dangling blue crystal earrings glistened in the sun

we shared ham and pineapple pizza
(what a surprise to discover you like it too)
and spread out our lives on the red checked table covering until it
was past closing time

we had taught
written books
and grieved for husbands who died

in time, you have taught me to dream horses
a dream I'll pass on to my great-granddaughters

now as Sunday mornings
come and go without you
I think of red day lilies

I remember
your silver-streaked hair, your willowy posture
as straight as an aspen sapling

you tell me you're well-cared for
in your hospice room
where flowers bloom outside the window

my heart
sends you larkspurs, sunflowers
and the cats we both love

my friend, you will live
in the cream and pink petals of our peace rose
and in Sunday morning music

For Jeanne Who Loved Back

Jeanne Whitehouse was a much-loved author of children's books including Sometimes I Dream Horses *and* I Have a Sister—My Sister Is Deaf.

You knew then, the last time we said goodbye
That death would take you before I came again
"Let's wait two more Saturdays, and then we'll see,"
You told me when I asked about abut my next visit
When I saw how much weaker you'd become
I should have known what "two more Saturdays" really meant

Perhaps I tried to hold on to you more tightly
Than even the strongest friendship can sustain
I texted a "thinking of you" message
Ending in a heart emoji
"Love you back." came your response
As brief as you had energy for
As brief as our time together

Before the second Saturday arrived
I lost you
Just after dawn
When you should have been in your garden
Grieving
I think of Walt Whitman's assurance
That "to die is different from
what anyone supposed and luckier."

Your oncologist's prediction:
Six months at most
But you fought to hold on for eight months
You who dreamed horses
Never complaining

Speaking well of the care you received in hospice
Thankful for friends who visited
Daughters who came to share with you
The last red and gold days of autumn

I brought you chicken salad sandwiches
Or pineapple chicken curry and other things you enjoyed
I covered your bedside table with a black and white checked cloth
Then tucked a red napkin under your chin
You smiled then ate so little, like a monk
Surviving on only a few grains of rice
After we ate, I read to you
For as long as you had energy to listen

Now, I will learn to dream horses
And think of you standing
As straight as an arrow shaft
A part of the universe of all things
Where I will meet you again
Someday

High Desert Evenings

The porch swing creeks
As we settle in, wine glasses in hand
To watch bees buzz
Among the leaves of the datura
Waiting for its blossoms to open

Like kids, impatient to see inside a package
We keep checking the time
Certain that by 8:00
Each of the white trumpet-shaped flowers,
Folded like a fan, will begin to pop open

As though the blossoms know
They're our evening's entertainment
Each one opens several seconds
After the one before
Their musky fragrance heady in the heat

When all the flowers have opened
We pour ourselves more wine
Then count them
Comparing the tally
To the plant's all-time record of 63

We sit for a while
Basking in the silence,
The fragrance, the wine
Grateful that on desert summer evenings
Miracles happen

Pronouns

We'll have four free days, you said
Your voice animated by the kind of enthusiasm
You usually reserve for hikes and wild creatures

We included me in the way I heard you say, we'll have
So I reveled in thinking about our spending them together
Failing to count on your revision of we'll to I'll

I didn't fall into a funk when you left on your motorcycle for one
of the four days
But I told you how I felt
Because, like a molehill, pronouns revised can grow into
mountains

I need let's and we'll defined in terms I can count on
You don't need to say them more often than you like
Just speak them accurately because they hold us in their meaning

Simple Things

There is nothing quite so simple as the rain
Not birth or death, though they should be
Beginning and ending as they are
Simple words
We start; we finish
Things we all understand

Nothing is quite as simple as rain baptizing leaves
Longing to be quenched by moisture so gentle
They can reassure themselves of the order of things
Inspired by the fine-tuned muse
Of the mind of God

Desperate Glory

Rain splotched my newly washed windows
And the little girl on the news hoped her brothers would kill
If they die, they'll go to heaven she said
Fifty-seven more died in a war
Backed by men who support surgical strikes
Though just how curing terror with terror might work
They cannot say

Like angel hair on a 50s Christmas tree
Blossoms cover the Rose of Sharon just outside my door
Their burgundy centers, a star in each white cup
Seeing them radiant in the waning sunlight
I cannot choose but ask:
How is it that the flowers beside my door continue to bloom
While the once fragrant morning of a woman I might have been
Reeks instead of artillery smoke and tissue torn asunder
By bombs strapped to bodies of children
Dying for some desperate glory?

Must rain always fall on newly washed windows?
And in the end, is death forever the cost of reaching heaven?

Without You

I'll plant tulips
For the second time since I buried you
Laid in the fertile earth
The simple things that defined us
Drives through the crisp autumn valley
Dinner where the young woman told us
She wants to be just like us
When she finds the right man
We danced by the fire late at night
Never guessing that one day
Dancing would give way
To separation so harsh and long
That not even in the mystery of our union
Can I hold on to you
I want to crush the days into pieces
And blow them like raindrops buffeted by a winter storm
Consign them to the emptiness my days are
Whenever I do the things we loved to do
Without you
The tulips I plant today
I plant for you
But they cannot bring gentle ease when spring comes
There is no resurrection without you

Wild Horses and Old Men

Like old men waiting for death or a welfare check
The ancient horses turn their bony flanks into the wind
Bracing themselves against gusts that come in desert springs
Biting as any winter storm they come
Winds that dry and toughen and deny
They wait for the bleached days of summer mirages
Promising rain that doesn't come to end their bone yard days

I have seen old men slouched into S's
Tied into wheelchairs; left beside their beds
I avoid their eyes seeking me from death's other kingdom
Their minds bound to images of mermaids
Their gnarled hands submissive

I think of the wizened wild horses
And dry wind blowing bleached summer days
Across chamisa and sand

Ariel's Wedding Poem

joy will come in the morning
when the sun shines softly
on your life together

the for better, for worse
of your love has grown
beyond the clatter of questions

your marriage will show you eternity
in the grains of sand
passing through the hourglass of your life

and joy will come
as your days unfold like morning glories
radiant and rare

Boundaries

Datura blossoms outside our bedroom door
Last an evening and a morning
By afternoon, their genes
Tell them to fold up like a fan
They bow their heads in the sun
Grateful for the boundaries they've been given
A day, no more, to perfume the air

This morning, after our first night together
I think about the moment when you realize
That within my embrace
Fall the contradictions of my failures at self-discipline
I do not will it so, but unlike the Daturas' boundaries
My genes designate the thrown-togetherness
I hope you will embrace

Crocuses and A Poem

last spring
the first crocus opened early
like the bright face of a child swinging in the park
its raucous yellow
gave way to a crocus riot that demanded
I come out to sit with them in silent sunlight
after an hour or so, my to-do list disappeared
leaving behind images I arranged into a poem
about sunflowers and the gold in my mother's hair

II. Haiku

Writing haiku in English once demanded strict counting of syllables: five, seven, five. Gratefully, that has changed. Now the most prominent journals, such as *Modern Haiku* look beyond syllable counting and focus on a more creative approach, publishing poems of two or even one line as well as a more traditional three lines. The one line is usually horizontal, but can be vertical. Often, the first and last images align with the middle of the poem. So what makes a fine haiku? The basic prerequisite involves the juxtaposition of two related images, often sense oriented, plus *kigo,* that is, the indication of a season. However, the absence of any of these things does not disqualify a particular haiku that is effective in other ways. Senryu is a form of haiku that is humorous, often focusing on human foibles. Most journals don't differentiate between the two.

Most haiku in *Counting the Ways* have appeared in various journals that focus on the form. My first published haiku is still one of my favorites, perhaps because it describes a scene from my childhood and includes my beloved Papa.

first melon
thump-ripe
Papa's pocket knife

clouds scud
across the full moon
daturas unfurl

the wind
kisses each stamen
white peony

our up-and-down
relationship
cactus flower

tip of the branch
an inchworm
touches the sun

Agnus Dei
the first rose
opens

a halo
on the half moon
coyotes howl

grandmother's
orange day lilies
all i know of her

tendrils
of gray hair
roots of an oak

walking path
a stranger touches me
with her smile

wheat shocks
shot through with sunlight
the palomino's mane

dust of snow
on a hemlock
how still the crow sits!

the wild horses
come for water
their frozen breath

fireside chat
another shot
of tequila

sunrise
a line of ants
on the melon

spring morning
letting it all hang out
sheets on the clothesline

the same old stories growing old

soft rain
throughout the night
her small hands

four-and-twenty
blackbirds sing
open mic

dinosaur fossil
the anger
we hold on to

wild poppies
along the highway
undocumented

mid june
our turtle appears at last
first tomato

relocation
of a flower pot
roly-polies unroll

xeriscape
counting
the ways

haute couture
at the growers' market
a lady bug

scent of lime trees
along the garden path
her brocade gown

growers' market
we take home
someone else's garden

magazines
in the surgeon's office
recipes cut out

church steeple
its dark shadow
on the park swings

super moon climbing the window screen
a spider

too much
pianissimo
soft snoring

cottonwood leaves
float by the window
"aire on a g string"

paupers' cemetery
only the clouds
come and go

a comment
for every occasion
mother-in-law's tongue

encased
in bubble wrap
painkillers

azalea branches
scratch against the screen
wolf moon

our cat snores
head upside down
state of the union

indian ponies
gallop across the mesa
blanket of wild verbenas

bees buzz
around the clover
taste of baklava

rows of crows
on the telephone wires
beauty salon gossip

the cellist
plays Rachmaninov
his yellow and blue socks

ebb tide
she asks about
his libido

an afterglow of gold
between the branches
dandelion wine

spring rain
the dimple
in her chin

words
i wish i hadn't said
icicles

morning sunlight
on the pond—
water-polished pebbles

toupee askew
if only we could see ourselves
as others do

his funeral
the cracker jacks box ring
i saved

a whiskey jay
lands on the cabin's roof
moonshine

a rusted metal horse
stands atop the hill
indian land

a black and white cat
sits on the welcome mat
houndstooth coat

the note you wrote
after our quarrel
paper cut

at the church door
she curls around her dog
silent night

buried
among pink violets
the fallen nestling

a pillow slips from
under the mall santa's shirt
fa-la-la-la-la

the explanation
rambles on and on
his adam's apple

end of an affair mid-winter snow on snow
on snow

apple tree buds
begin to swell
the question in his eyes

juneteenth
what we still refuse
to talk about

III. Haibun

Haibun, a form Matsuo Basho, a seventeenth century poet created, combines narrative prose and haiku related to the story line.

Paper Bags

                        full moon
                        lights the climbing rose
                        her red hair

"You have to stop acting like a tomboy," my mother drawls, drawing out vowels in a wind chime voice. "There's another hole in the sole of your left shoe."

She traces my foot on a piece of cardboard, cuts around the outline, and places the new sole inside my shoe. "We have to save for rent and food." Her hands feel soft when she touches my face.

Spending time inside with my mother makes me feel liked I'm closed inside a paper bag. Going with Papa to milk the cows rips it open. He lets me slip the milking machines onto their teats.

The feel of their pink and white udders reminds me of my mother's silk slip. And of her touch.

                        queen Anne's lace
                        the wedding pearls
                        saved for me

Belongings

Bent almost double, she pushes a grocery cart. It holds her
    belongings, except a coat. She drapes its hood over her head,
    hiding her face.

She stumbles along, feet half in, half out of someone else's shoes

                                    hand-me-downs
                                    her arms
                                    shorter than mine

Things Not Understood

                    bricks of mud and straw
                    dry in the sun
                    house raising

The gravel crunches as we trudge up a path leading to the narrow *morada*. Bits of straw in the building's deteriorating adobe bricks glisten in the sun. We pause to think of flagellants sacrificing themselves for the sins of their neighbors in remote villages where there is no priest to hear confession.

                    on a hill
                    three wooden crosses
                    silence

The *morada's* boarded door and windows speak to the secrecy of the Brotherhood who re-enact a version of the crucifixion during Holy Week. Today, processions in which the Brothers drag heavy crosses on their backs replace the re-enactments.

In their initiation rites, a Brother washes the candidate's feet. Then incisions in the shape of the cross are cut into his shoulder.

                    blossoms
                    of the redbud tree
                    Good Friday

The wind howls as we walk around the building, an eerie reminder of the alabados the men sing and of their cries as the thorns of yucca fronds bite into their flesh.

                                              a dust devil
                                              obscures our vision
                                              whispered prayer

Papa Married an Anglo

My father planted rutabagas because my mother loved them. Mama mashed them with butter and stirred in chopped green chile. "*Que bueno,*" Papa would say, tempting me when I turned up my nose at their turnipy taste.

                                  wedding pearls
                                  passed on to me
                                  my dark skin

A New Nose

                                            in the mirror
                                            the high cost
                                            of living

"It's malignant," the voice on the phone tells me.

I arrive for surgery the following morning. Numbing injections. The first causes tearing up. Then injections two, three, four and so on. By the time the surgeon is ready to start, I'm sure he could decapitate me.

"I'll remove the tumor a layer at a time and look at each under the microscope until I'm sure the cancer is gone," the doctor explains. "I won't take more than I absolutely have to so that rebuilding your nose won't be too much of a problem."

"Fantastic," I tell myself. "A new nose. Maybe it'll look better than the one I've seen in the mirror for eighty years."

                                            jousting
                                            at windmills
                                          the surgeon's scalpel

The Witness

                                      a cracker jacks box
                                      engagement ring
                                      his red convertible

The three of us drive across the open border between El Paso and Juarez to find a justice of the peace we've heard will marry us. I'm sixteen.

My cat Blackie squirms in my arms as we climb the stairs to the judge's office. "It's okay," I tell him and scratch his ears. The stairwell reeks of smoke and urine.

David hands the sour-faced judge $25.00. He pockets our money then asks, "Where are your witnesses?" Panicked, I turn to the judge's wife. "*Por favor, Señora,* will you help us?"

"*Si, mija,* she responds She takes Blackie and tells her husband, "The cat and I are the witnesses." Blackie purrs as we say, "I do."

                                      45 years
                                    the liver transplant
                                    comes too late

Desperation

She sits on the median, hunched over a puppy. A blanket drapes over the two of them.

No "Need Help" sign. Just terrified eyes. I give her my lunch and the little cash I have.

                                    huddled
                                    against the church door
                                    they sit in silence

The Gamble

>   we elope
>   to Juarez
>   i'm sixteen

"It will be a crap shoot," the doctor who will perform David's transplant tells us. He sees the confusion on our faces and continues. "There are more people needing livers than there are donors. This means, we wait until patients are near death before scheduling a transplant."

"He doesn't deserve to die from hepatitis C that he has because of a transfusion. You can't be serious!" My voice escalates to a near-scream.

The hospital room into which David is finally admitted is cold. I sit beside his bed where he has lain for two days. We talk about what we'll do once he's recovered. The surgeon comes in. "We've decided David can't survive a transplant. I'm sorry."

My husband loses consciousness. I climb into his bed and put my head on his shoulder.

>   don't be afraid
>   i say over and over
>   my heart knows he hears

Veterans' Home

Tied in wheelchairs, the old men slouch into S's. I smile as I help their gnarled hands position straws to drink from cups of water. Their blank eyes stare at me.

>ward D
>images of mermaids
>beckon in dreams

As I move among the men, I'm reminded of the ancient horses that come to our house in the hills above the city. We keep a tank of water filled to allow them to slake their thirst. Like old men waiting for death or a welfare check, the wild horses bow their heads to drink.

>dry winds whirl
>across chamisa and sand
>another mirage

Just the Two of Us

We hike to a rocky outcropping to say our vows. You play "The Rose" on your harmonica. I read a poem I've written.

We sit in silence, watching two birds circling close by. "Our witnesses," we say. For a moment, I remember my mother's wedding dress.

                         a string of pearls
                         hidden away—
                         white hydrangeas

The Promises They Made

She gazes up at him from her wheelchair. "I'm told I'll never walk again."

"If you'll trust me, I'll help you stand," my father says reaching out to her. His eyes hold hers as she struggles to her feet, her auburn hair falling into her face. "One day soon, you'll walk," he promises.

When they elope, she wears a green crepe dress to walk by his side.

>   she paces the floor
>   patting the baby's back
>   their auburn hair

IV. Tankas

Tankas consist of five lines. Its language is sense-oriented imagery, similar to haiku, but may contain figurative language such as similes or metaphors. The poems contain two seeming unrelated events, images, or ideas brought together, often in an unexpected way. The shift usually occurs after the first three lines. Tankas portray human relationships or the author's situation. In the words of Sanford Goldstein, "behind the scene is the autobiographical moment of the poet."

like a mind reader
you know when i need you
to play your harmonica
your hands
brighten the days for me

campaign promises
so easily made
as easily broken
the jack-o-lantern
snickers

letters signed
i love you
not in papa's hand
mother's
keepsake box

full moon
lights the house
how deep the quiet!
the cricket
has found its mate

the massage therapist
searches for the right places
to soothe my soreness
like a lullaby
her hands lull me to sleep

like a subtle perfume
the fragrance of moon flowers
lights the way to romance
at twilight
the cicada calls its mate

just before falling asleep
i remember Hemingway's words:
strong in all the broken places
my addict friend's
struggle to recover

dust rises
like smoke signals
from the banks of the rio grande
catfish skeletons embedded
where water once flowed

unannounced
the quiet hours
slip in
learning to read
sitting in papa's lap

a new day lily
the color of wine
if only i could make
each of my days
as remarkable

outside the grocery store
the Salvation Army lady
rings her bell
belief in
promises made

a wake-up call
before the alarm
like a kitten's whiskers
your soft hands
brush against my cheek

infinity
counting the ways
you say "I love you."
morning coffee
planting red tulips

About the Author

Sharon Rhutasel-Jones retired after half a century of teaching and became a writer. She's published two books: *Living by Ear: Memoir of a Wayward Teacher* and *The Teacher Who Learned from Cats.* Her short poetry appears in various journals, her longer poems in anthologies including *Bearing the Mask, Weaving the Terrain,* and *New Mexico Poetry Anthology.*

She lives in a village near the Rio Grande with her husband Larry and their cat Danny Boy. When not writing, she gardens and plays the piano. She loves to cook, often using recipes published in *The New York Times* as well as those she's saved in notebooks over the years.

www.ingramcontent.com/pod-product-compliance
Lightning Source LLC
Chambersburg PA
CBHW031159160426
43193CB00008B/442